A BUCKET OF OIL

**The Humanistic Approach
to Building Design
for Energy Conservation**

William Wayne Caudill

Frank D. Lawyer

Thomas A. Bullock

Cahners Books

Library of Congress Catalog Card Number: 74-789

International Standard Book Number: 0-8436-0126-4

Printed in the United States of America

Comment

Despite warnings over the years from high places the energy crisis shocks us all. Typically we react by clamoring for more, bigger and different sources of energy. For the first time we start seriously to explore the heat of the sun, the power of the winds and the rains, the warmth of the earth, the chemistry of the atom — wherever we may find and capture energy from sources available, renewable and infinite.

Typically, too, while we await the development of new sources we restrain ourselves as consumers. Mostly we do this by exhortation: use less of everything to avoid rationing until power flows copiously again.

Meanwhile, back at the buildings, there are some things we can do that are prudent whether or not low cost energy ever returns. They are things which should be done if we care very much about how our grandchildren live out their lives on this "one inhabited star".

The lively authors of this book suggest a multitude of measures which, taken together, can move our buildings, especially for education, toward a more human and ecological design. They ask us to rethink the profligate ways we have sought comfort and amenity, to examine the options still open to us, to update our facts and our feelings about what constitutes physical well-being. Standards for ventilation comfort and safety, for example, that still are influenced by "research" conducted before the turn of the century, linger on. Thus today's expensive enchantment with "fresh" air.

The authors recognize how plural our people are; that almost nothing will be true everywhere. Yet most of the ideas presented here will be applicable somewhere, all to the end that our buildings will grace the land, praise our culture, and by their nature be not only good neighbors to the earth but sensible consumers of its bounty. Only then will people be able to afford their never-ending quest for comfort.

The main thrust of this book is to return to fundamentals as we retreat from affluence and the spendthrift days of energy unlimited. The senior author of "A Bucket of Oil", when complimented for a career marked by high imagination, once replied, "I never invented anything until I first got in a mess".

It could be that out of the energy mess will come a host of new ways to bring comfort to people. If so, this is a good beginning.

Dr. Harold B. Gores, President
Educational Facilities Laboratories, Inc.
New York City
March 1974

Thanks

We are grateful to Dr. James R. Wright, Mr. James L. Haecker, and Mr. Frank J. Powell, Center for Building Technology, Institute for Applied Technology, National Bureau of Standards, for their assistance in providing technical information, guidance, and many helpful suggestions.

CRS *Bucket of Oil* Team

Editorial: Jan Talbot and Susan Kent Caudill
Graphic Design: Robert Lane
Technology: D. Kirk Hamilton
Production: J. Lindy Pollard
Printing: Wall Company Inc.

Consultants

Engineering: Joe B. Thomas
Building Systems: Jonathan King
Solar Collectors: Michel Bezman

CRS Energy Conservation Committee

James B. Gatton
Charles E. Lawrence
Neil Madeley
William M. Peña
Joe B. Thomas
Michael H. Trower

All of the drawings were done by Frank Lawyer. All buildings shown in the photographs were designed by the Caudill Rowlett Scott team and its associates.

How to Find What You Want

In this energy crisis we need to remind ourselves that it takes two to make architecture happen— a person and a building. And in that order. People are more important than their buildings. Architecture—not the building itself or the art and science of designing it—is a personal, enjoyable, necessary experience. Man perceives and appreciates form and space from three distinctly different but interrelated attitudes: of the physical being, of the emotional being, and of the intellectual being. When architecture does happen to this person, an aura seems to emanate from form and space that evokes an emotional response by fulfilling his physical, emotional and intellectual needs. We know that if these needs are not fulfilled, man's behavioral patterns are affected. Our challenge for the future is to conserve energy, yes. But we must at at the same time preserve the dignity of man.

The Humanistic Approach to Building Design for Energy Conservation

Oil is our new scare word. The symbol of another national, international crisis.

How are we going to keep warm in winter, cool in summer? What will happen to our life style? What will happen to all of us—poor or rich—when the well runs dry?

So many questions. At first too few answers. And then too much crisis and panic-produced thinking.

We think this is one crisis we already have a handle on in architecture. It's both too soon and too late to panic. Who are we? We are members of the CRS (Caudill Rowlett Scott) team, an interdisciplinary group that has been together 27 years trying to design and construct better buildings.

Energy, people and their buildings. That's what this book is all about. Throughout you will find these underlying premises: 1) Buildings today waste energy; 2) through proper design the wasted energy can be saved; 3) energy shapes buildings; 4) buildings shape the way people live, work and play; 5) energy can be saved without sacrificing esthetic and human values.

The energy crisis will obviously force us to cut back. The point is we can use less energy and still have buildings, even better buildings, whose forms and spaces possess architecture.

Buildings consume an incredible amount of energy, about one third of all the energy used in this country. The U.S. National Bureau of Standards people, who are on top of building technology and know what it's all about, say that about forty percent of that energy is wasted. For those of you who like to visualize numbers, that's 65 billion gallon buckets of oil each year wasted. That's also 65 billion gallon buckets of oil that can be saved if we go about things in the right way.

Frankly, we got suckered into some of the mess we're in today, and not just by the relative amount of oil in the world and our ability to get it. The design profession picked up sloppy methods during the affluent 60's. Our firm, too. If our clients said they wanted all glass walls on the west, our engineers proudly replied: "We can do anything you want done, even make you comfy in a glass box." They were right. All they needed was some cheap fuel. We didn't have this attitude in the fifties. "More is better" crept up on us without our really knowing it. We began to like the superfluous, which we had hated. Buildings in the United States became obese. And did they eat energy!

What can be done? The obvious is to change the "more is better" attitude. We can't go on doing everything people want just because technology makes it possible. Energy is community property. We've learned that the hard way. A bad building which guzzles energy steals from its neighbors. With our attitude back in shape, we can do a better designing job.

That's what this book is about, too. Learning to design buildings to do their job without guzzling energy. Creating a Cadillac building with a Volkswagen engine. Cutting out that 40 percent waste factor.

We are after economy, defined at CRS as "maximum results with minimum means". But we must also realize that economy of energy concerns human life and human values. We are not giving up on the quality of life to save energy. Rather, we must re-think our life style in terms of energy conservation and other human values. When we spend energy, we want no waste. And when we spend energy, we want full value in return.

We can learn how to save energy—how best to use a bucket of oil. We have the technology. Can we learn to fulfill the needs of the human being at the same time?

Let's go back thirty years. We had oil and gas rationing. We knew what to do when we had no fuel readily available. We walked and used streetcars to get to work. We shut off heat in rooms except those with southern exposure to save oil—simple as that. We put the baby crib in the south bedroom. The sun coming in through the windows did most of the heating. The baby was comfortable during very cold days with no oil-generated heat at all—only the heat from the sun. And in the coldest climates. We have past lessons as well as more flexibility than present day living standards suggest for saving energy.

Let's go back twenty five years. The CRS team designed a so-called "solar house" in Oklahoma City. It wasn't sun powered with solar collectors, nor was it like the U.S. General Services Administration's energy conservation demonstration building in Manchester, New Hampshire, the University of Delaware Solar One house or Prototype One in New Mexico. A solar house back then was one which had a lot of glass to capture the winter sun and a lot of overhangs to keep the sun off during hot summer months—elementary but fundamental. In our solar house, fuel was saved all year round. Part of what we must do in this new energy crisis is not new at all.

After our so-called solar house, the CRS team made its reputation designing little naturally lighted and naturally ventilated schoolhouses. Economy was what we were after then. The sun and wind were used to save money—not fuel. We argued that light from the sun cost a lot less than light from the power plant. That it took a hell of a big fan to generate air flow to duplicate the effect of a comforting five mile an hour breeze. During these years of saving money by saving fuel, we learned much about the way certain buildings behave under different sky and wind conditions. In fact, we developed some fairly sophisticated methods to predetermine natural lighting and ventilation. The wind tunnel and sky dome at Texas A & M University were kept busy testing models for architects and engineers throughout the U.S. and other countries.

We found how to bounce light off the ground into deep, interior spaces; how to cut building costs by decreasing the perimeter and lowering ceilings, yet have quality natural lighting; how to funnel the cooling wind around the people who use our buildings; how to design pressure walls to ventilate leeward spaces, even reversing the direction of the wind and increasing the velocity. We also learned how to modify the outdoors with wind breaks and sun pockets, using the outside for functional activities. The key is control. And some controls we already know how to use.

The point is simple. Now is the time to recapture knowledge of natural ventilation and natural lighting. We need to be able to design supplementary systems for mechanical and electrical systems—in case the well runs dry.

Is the design profession ready? We know it's technologically possible to design and build energy saving buildings. Whether that will happen is a tough question. Certainly complacency exists in the profession. But there are many outstanding individuals and firms of architects, engineers and planners who are responding to the energy crisis.

In our own firm there is a wonderful atmosphere of excitement about being part of a movement which will result in a new era of building design. We get excited thinking about bringing in new kinds of buildings and new forms of cities. We want a chance to demonstrate what we can do to conserve energy and serve human values. We are capable of responding to the energy crisis if given a chance to innovate.

One problem is codes. Building codes. If the government starts imposing legalized restrictions on creativity, we're sunk. Government decisions—state and federal—will soon be made, significantly affecting how well the design profession will be able to respond to the energy crisis. What is at stake—what kind of codes the several states will have—is important both in and outside of the design profession. It's important for the energy crisis.

Prescription codes are the enemy. We're certainly not opposed to building codes designed to protect health and safety. This isn't the issue. What we fear is a different kind of code. Two kinds need mention here.

Prescription codes prescribe exactly how something is to be done. Exactly how a building must be built. It's like telling a carpenter he can pound a nail only from a north-northeast angle. Or telling an artist a painting can have only two colors. It's strictly arbitrary. Once the reason behind the prescription code becomes invalid, say through an advance in building technology or a new idea, it makes no sense. But, "It's the law. Do it." We should tell you here that the authors and their partners are "battle scarred bastards" who have fought code wars in nearly every state of the United States. Lost most of them. Won a few. But damn few.

Performance codes, the lesser of evils if we must have codes beyond health and safety protection, dictate what result should be achieved without specifying how to do it. Creativity is at least possible with performance codes.

In November 1973 we attended a Washington, D.C. meeting sponsored by the National Conference of States on Building Codes and Standards working with the Center for Building Technology of the National Bureau of Standards (NBS). The purpose of the meeting was to evaluate a model federal code then in the works which recognized energy conservation. The federal code is only a model. The individual states, which have the legal authority to pass building codes, are expected to come up with their own codes beginning in 1974.

That meeting is responsible for this book because what we heard there scared the hell out of us.

Both sponsoring groups, particularly the people in NBS Center for Building Technology, have done a superb job providing alternatives to prescription codes, putting in their place performance codes which encourage, not stifle, creativity. And during the meeting we were greatly impressed with their systematic approach to developing guides.

Things were going great at the meeting for awhile. Then, wham. Someone got up and recommended inserting this provision: "Windows in housing projects should not exceed 15 percent of the total wall area." A prescription code. No validity. Strictly arbitrary. Then one man sitting next to us said, "That's too much. We've got to get rid of these damn glass buildings." That wasn't so bad, but he also said, "The permissible use of glass should be half that." He got a hand of applause. Overreaction at its worst. This sort of thinking would set us back to the dark ages of architectural practice.

What we are saying is that function, beauty and economy can go down the drain along with energy if we are tied to prescription codes. And this is a loss we do not have to suffer because of the energy crisis.

Two cases in point: What happened to us as designers, and to the people who live and work in our buildings, when even a fairly good idea was translated into a prescription code with the force of law?

First: The more space you have the more energy you need to heat and cool. Makes sense. Yet at least six states in which we built schools passed prescription codes that dictated excessive volume. We encountered this money-wasting regulation first in Texas in the early 50's. The Texas School Building Law from which this requirement came was passed in 1913—on the books nearly forty years. Because of it, millions of dollars in public tax money was wasted. What it actually said was this: "No part of the said classroom or study hall shall be at a greater distance from the window than twice the height of the top of the window above the floor." Most school teachers would like their classrooms to be at least 28 feet wide, preferably 30. If so, the ceiling would have to be 14 feet high or 15 in the latter case. That's excessive volume—nearly one third more than necessary. The more volume, the more energy.

Second: In a north central state a few years ago, we proposed a highly compact "cold weather schoolhouse". Our clients, the local school board, the teachers and the children, loved the plan. It was circular. The library was the axle for two rings of classrooms. Our heating engineers particularly loved it because it had minimum outside walls. In our estimate we saved 27 percent outside wall over conventional schools built in the state at that time. That would cut the heating load substantially, reducing both the initial cost of the building and later operating costs. What happened? State officials turned it down flat. "Regulations state clearly that each classroom must have windows. Skylights won't do," they said. What a great building that would have been —with minimum energy input. We lost the battle. The state got a school. But one that was thirty years old before it was off the drafting board. Today energy is being wasted in that school because of a damnfool regulation.

Parenthetically, one of the most satisfying experiences we had in our long war of combating prescription codes happened just a few years ago in a southern state. The code read something like this: "The amount of glass area should not exceed the area of the largest wall." Admittedly we pulled a dirty. We again submitted a circular building. It drove the code police bananas.

If we are going to have to live with codes, we prefer performance codes. We have a lot of respect for the people who worked up the model federal code. If anyone can come up with a "good" code,

11

they can. But what will happen when each state comes up with its own version?

And, in a sense, even a "good" code is not what we need for the design profession to have a productive, efficient, creative response to the energy crisis. We need freedom to design so we can build highly functional, people-oriented buildings requiring less energy.

To conserve energy, we need to work with principles. And working with principles is a process of re-discovery, not invention. There are principles of design which are as valid today as when the three of us were teaching college architecture years ago. We believe each has as its foundation an underlying principle: function, economy and form are one. And economy includes the economy of energy. By using the following principles which underscore the energy component, we form the basis for designing to conserve energy.

Orientation: If we're careful how we place the building on the site, we can save energy.

Solar heat control: Heat from the sun flows into a building by radiation, convection and conduction. This heat source can be controlled to reduce the amount of energy required to heat and cool a building.

Solar light control: Daylighting saves energy.

Task recognition: When the different heating, cooling and lighting requirements for specific tasks to be done within a building are recognized and acknowledged, savings in energy will result.

Efficiency: Less energy will be required if a building does its job with minimum floor area.

Regionalism: Recognition of a specific region— the climate, terrain, natural growth and local mores—leads to energy conservation.

Wind: Wind will help or hinder physical comfort. Directing and modifying the wind on and within a building can save energy.

Heat flow: When heat flow is caused by conduction, insulation is required to stop it; when heat flow is caused by radiation, a reflective material is required to stop it; and when heat flow is caused by convection, a vacuum or "dead air space" is needed; and, conversely, to cause heat to flow, we take away insulation, the reflecting material, or dead air space.

Conditioned outdoors: If you condition outdoor space by modifying the effects of sun, wind and rain to reduce the inside area, there will be substantial energy savings.

Controls: The ability to cut off the energy flow to certain sections of the building when not in use offers energy saving opportunities.

Comfort: Temperature tolerances differ among various regions. Social, economic background, age, as well as physical make-up of each individual also affect temperature tolerance of the individual. Accordingly comfort standards for all people lose their validity.

Centralization vs. decentralization: Whether the building plant or the heating/cooling system is centralized or decentralized depends upon each individual situation. Neither alternative should be ruled out.

Building geometry: The shape of a building can conserve energy.

Esthetics: A person appreciates a building when he is satisfied physically, emotionally and intellectually. All three must be there because people are never only physical, only emotional, or only intellectual in actual experience. Intellectual understanding of architecture can influence how people react to cold temperatures in a room and vice versa. People will leave a room, for example, that is ugly, cold or confusing, sometimes without knowing exactly which reaction led them to the door. Physical comfort cannot be separated from esthetic comfort.

What's beauty these days? Let's zero in on this last principle. The energy crisis has already changed the notion of beauty. It's difficult to see beauty in buildings that have an inherent craving for energy. The highly admired complex forms of the 60's are losing their eye appeal, too, because people are beginning to realize that the juts, zigzags and extravagant use of outside walls are inefficient forms for saving energy. A new morality of form is emerging.

We need lean and clean buildings. The architecture of excessiveness must be replaced with an architecture of economy—economy of natural resources and materials as well as energy. The architectural revolution near the beginning of the century responded to an intellectual change among philosophers, artists, architects and engineers. We're due for another revolution in architecture which responds to the attitudinal changes of all people about fuel shortages as well as the total environmental, conservation picture. When someone fights to save a tree or a view, he's ready to fight to save any natural resource. This unquestionably affects his concept of beauty.

Architecture cannot be looked upon as the art of self expression of the creative designer. It's too important to people—all people. Buildings must be responsive to humans and human environment. That's why the people who will use our buildings are included on our design teams.

The energy crisis—together with the conservation movement—could have much more impact on building design than the great "form givers" of the last three decades: Frank Lloyd Wright, Le Corbusier, Mies van der Rohe and Louis Kahn.

Personal expression, excessiveness and exhibitionism are on the way out. Beauty will be found in logical solutions to the problems of conserving natural resources. A recognition of past strengths as well as mistakes shows us there is no need to sacrifice beauty or practicality in the architecture that grows out of the energy crisis and the environmental movement.

Six simple guidelines can save energy. Saving energy is complex. There are hundreds of variables that need simultaneous consideration. But underlying this complexity are simple guidelines to be used in making design decisions. If you grasp these, you have the essence of energy control relating to building design.

1. Use the climate. Put the elements to work.

2. Make the envelope—the outside structure of the building—lean and clean. The more walls and roof area, the more energy it takes.

3. Design lighting systems for specific tasks.

4. Design on the edge of comfort zones. People can wear more or less clothing to suit individual comfort needs.

5. Use energy efficient systems—cooling/ heating, lighting, wall/roof components and fenestration, the relation of wall openings which let in air, light and view.

6. Provide controls, automatic or on-off switches, so energy can be saved when spaces are not in use or when systems need modification.

We have a profusion of energy-saving techniques. We've already talked about natural heating and lighting systems using outside air, wind and sun. By considering the site, orientation of the building, the envelope, electrical, mechanical and plumbing systems, we can derive the specifics which follow the design guidelines and principles.

Consider the site. Put trees to work to shelter buildings from unwanted hot sun and cold blowing wintry winds. If on a hillside, bury part of the building. What better insulation! Below the frost line, ground temperature is fairly constant. Avoid combination of wind and low temperature; avoid light and heat reflections from other buildings, surfaces, water or ground. Be careful about

13

wind paths, pressure effects and how wind behaves over topography or around nearby buildings. Think twice before putting buildings on stilts in cold climates.

Consider the envelope. Think in terms of minimum temperature difference from outside to inside. Keep the floor area to a minimum. Remember that heat flows both ways through a wall, so use plenty of insulation to stop it. Place insulated walls with the least glass toward the worst weather (generally north). Also avoid glass on the hot west exposures. Use double glass, tinted and reflective, to stop heat transfer, but remember it also stops winter benefits of sun. Minimize air leakage on the envelope and respect the winds which blow through cracks. So caulk, seal, and damper. Take advantage of wall mass—the holding power of cold and heat. Remember a window is a control to be used as a control for thermal and visual comfort. Use shading for windows in summer, permitting sun penetration in winter. Use light colors inside and out. Use vapor barriers. Insulate edges of foundations and slab floors. Use outdoor air at night to pre-cool in summer. Avoid hot or cold surfaces near seated people (we use peripheral halls called thermal zones to do this; walking people can take more heat and more cold). Design vertical shafts that leak little air. Use open plans that allow transfer of excess heat between the utility core and the periphery of a building. Open plans (not eggcrate arrangements) have less heat loss and more illumination. Arrange and size spaces for minimum use of elevators. Use unheated stairs and corridors. Locate public traffic on the first floor to minimize energy-consuming equipment such as escalators. Make use of outdoor lobbies and social courts. Don't heat underground garages unless waste heat is used. Keep entrance lobbies out of the wind. Think of the total envelope as one wall having a specified "U" factor, a measure of how quickly the heat will go or not go through the wall.

Consider systems. Use high efficiency fans and low pressure loss ducts. Use heat exchangers to recover heat from exhaust air to heat incoming cold air. Treat and recirculate indoor air using a minimum of outdoor air for odor control. Use evaporative cooling when possible.

Eliminate air leakage from ducts. Insulate ducts in non-conditioned spaces and where they pass through conditioned spaces. Eliminate all re-heat requiring new energy to the systems. Use an economizer cycle, but do it right. We used one in Colorado, but because the main duct is open when outside air is brought in, everything freezes. We now know how to pinch down the opening to keep the coils from freezing.

People will live downtown again. Now let's "jump the scale" as we say in the drafting room. Let's go from thinking about details such as insulating heating ducts, to the larger scale of planning a central business district. We manage the scale jump quite well because in CRS we design everything from drapery fabrics to cities.

It's clear by now we think the energy shortage can be a good thing if it slows us down long enough to think about what we're doing and how we live. Many families now live in single-family homes twenty miles from work. The man or woman drives to work alone while the other spouse takes the second car to the neighborhood shopping center (which advertises thirty acres of parking as its main attraction). The kids take the third car to school. We can no longer accept so much wasteful energy consumption.

One of two things will happen, probably both: People will huddle more. They will move closer to work, and work will move closer to home. The downtowns of our cities will remain centers of activity, and the range of activities there will expand. People will live downtown again, walking or riding some form of mass transit. The inner city will have a new vitality, sparked by a return to urban living.

Multi-use buildings will come into play. The term "office building" may go out of use. Why use a building for only one function? We'll have buildings and building complexes that are multi-use. People will live, work, plan, do everything we do over hundreds of square miles in most cities, but in one building or group of buildings. Downtown will be a 24-hour instead of an 8-hour place. Some urban spaces will be outdoors or partly outdoors, naturally ventilated and lighted. In a few years, crossing a downtown street may mean using a bridge two hundred feet above ground. CRS has already built a few crossovers in the central business district, over the street and below the street. That expression Central Business District will probably be passe soon, too. The center of the city will not be just for business, but also for education, recreation, sports, and religion.

Downtown will be car-less. The car gets picked on a lot in energy conscious-environmental circles because it's the most visible symbol of conspicuous consumption. It uses energy inefficiently, in terms of moving people from point A to point B. It requires large amounts of land for streets, highways and parking lots and it has bad breath.

We can remove the car from downtown by eliminating the need for it. The multi-use complex and intra-urban mass transit will mean we can rely on walking or the modern equivalent of the streetcar for transportation.

We'll have interurban mass transit if we need to go to another city two hundred miles away. The public transportation system there will eliminate the need to rent a car upon arrival. The automobile isn't going to disappear, but we will use less of them.

Airports and aircraft will change. The modern airport is another conspicuous consumer of resources, especially land. Since present-day airplanes make a lot of noise, we build our airports miles from residential neighborhoods and the central business district. Sometimes we spend as much time driving to the airport as we do in flight. While aeronautical engineering isn't our thing, we hope technological development will lead to more efficient aircraft and airports.

We'll be staying home more. We'll be getting around within and between cities in new, more efficient ways, but maybe not as much, because we'll be able to do all the things we need to do at home. Our suburbs will reflect the new lifestyle but with less density than downtown. Future single-family units will be linked together to form total communities. Community commons will replace the fenced-in yard. Schools, stores, and offices will be within walking distance or reached by a suburban transit system. We won't have megastructures but we will consolidate. Bedroom communities will become complete towns and villages. The home itself will be part of a group sharing heating/cooling plants and utilities with other residences. The detached single-family home as we know it will disappear.

New energy sources. Solar energy systems for homes, groups of homes and other buildings and building complexes may reach widespread use. Conservationists and environmentalists are pushing the use of solar energy now at least partly in reaction to plans for widespread use of the more costly, more dangerous nuclear plants which have sparked controversy throughout the country. Hardware manufacturing and delivery systems are not now available. But private citizens, developers and school officials are going through private contractors to experiment with and develop solar systems. Several manufacturers expect to market solar systems very soon. So we will have some alternative heating systems in addition to those that depend on oil.

Plan the land. For the first time in American history, the public is beginning to favor land controls, without thinking that such regulations are against the whole system of free enterprise and private property. Both mass transit and the 24-hour, multi-use complex will help us to use our resources more effectively, and land use planning will become one of our most important tools. How we use land is just as important as how we use energy. Both are finite resources, yet our sprawling cities have jumped over large blocks of land that could be developed much more efficiently. Where land is really limited, we may use underground construction techniques and build below the streets. Underground spaces will be easy to heat and cool, too.

People will build in a different way. There's a lot of waste and inefficiency in the traditional construction process. Architects and contractors are going to learn to work with building components produced in a factory and delivered to the site ready for assembly. Factory built components don't waste materials. One of the major short-term aspects of the energy problem is a shortage of construction material. By designing and building with factory produced components we complete buildings more efficiently and use less energy doing it.

Space-age technology is needed. As designers, we foretell what a building is going to look like, how it's going to work and what effects it will have on the people who live and work there. We do everything to help the client visualize his building before construction ever starts. We do this with analysis cards, hundreds of sketches and measured drawings, and models. It works fairly well—on simple buildings.

Five years ago we started making the computer a tool for automating the complex aspects of the design process. At first it was used mostly to handle engineering aspects, particularly the design of structural frames. Later, we added the mechanical and electrical aspect of design. Then we set up programs for cost control and construction management. More recently we added

the architectural programming for analysis of functional needs. Now, with the energy crunch and the immediate goal to design buildings with optimum energy consumption, accurate prognostication is still the key. All we have to do, at least in our firm as well as in many others, is to keep on going the way we're going.

The computer program CRS now has in use is what we call EAP (Energy Analysis Program). It is updated and in tune with energy conservation. In essence, EAP is an automated process that enables us to accurately predetermine and control the impact our design solutions will have on the operating and cost efficiency of our clients' buildings. It deals with initial costs of buildings and long-range or life-cycle cost. EAP consists of four program modules: weather data analysis, heating/cooling load, energy requirements and operating cost. Continuing development of EAP will focus on providing new dimensions for system selection by analyzing capital, maintenance and replacement costs, as well as operating energy cost data now available.

In short, CRS has the technological know-how and the tools to use as little of that bucket of oil as possible. And we know there are many other firms in the design profession with similar capabilities. We hope the government will not pass codes which restrict us from innovative use of space age technology in designing efficient, energy saving buildings.

Build computer models. Computer models help us to obtain a total perspective of energy consumption. Just as we have always made scale models from chipboard to help us visualize form and function, so this computer energy analysis program permits us to build models to evaluate energy input with different design solutions. Imagine turning a building on its axis 360 points of the compass to test the energy pull of each orientation. The model also helps designers in other ways, from choosing the kind of glass to selecting the most logical heating system. The CRS team thinks the computer is the greatest thing since the invention of chipboard. But the computer alone is not our pass to new energy consciousness.

What the computer can't do. The computer can't make judgments, for one thing. It can feed the design team information to make these judgments. But it can't tell the design team whether to sacrifice a magnificent view to save a bucket of oil. That's the designer's decision. And this is where we can run into trouble—finding a balance between saving energy and fulfilling basic human needs. Consider the sun as one example. It can be gentle or rough. It can provide perfect light for reading or be blinding. It can warm you when you are cold or make you too hot on a summer day. We know and can measure these thermal and lighting effects.

But what about the psychological effects? They matter, too. Think how you feel when the sun appears after days of overcast. A little sunlight can turn you on. It can extend the edge of your personal comfort zone. Our experience has shown that teachers and children prefer south over north classrooms because "they are cheerful". Even the computer can't measure cheerfulness.

The pure scientific approach won't do. It's true we have engineering tables to tell us that 80 percent of a certain group of people tested feel comfortable under certain conditions. That's still loose, but at least we're getting close to what is physical comfort. But physical comfort is all mixed with emotional and intellectual comfort. We have to add a strong humanistic perspective to our approach to save energy. And we can. It's only practical.

The goal is a balance between supply and demand with a notion of demand that goes far beyond the economic to a broad range of human values. We can't save a bucket of oil at any cost,

because we can't live in windowless, but highly efficient boxes. Our chief concern is to fulfill the real needs of people. Those of us who have been designing buildings for years and evaluating how people live in them know that the emotional and intellectual needs are for real.

It takes a humanistic approach. We must think of our buildings as facilities to enrich life—not boxes for storing people. Saving energy must become a design determinant. But human values must be design determinants, too.

We must innovate to save those buckets of oil, but we must not trade off man. In the next section, you will see how the CRS team has attempted to find balance through a humanistic approach in designing buildings for optimum energy use. Thumb through the pages. Or skip to photos and sketches which interest you. There is no sequence. The kind of approach we propose is not linear. It is omnidirectional. We strongly believe that the traditional approach to design from one perspective must give way to an omnidirectional approach from many perspectives.

We hope the following photos and sketches give evidence to this humanistic approach.

How do we measure the total effect of a sunbeam? We can tell how much it heats a wall. Or how many footcandles it provides on a certain task surface. But what does it really do to a person? What does it do to a plant on the windowsill—to the person who wants the plant to live and grow? What happens to the atmosphere as the scattered clouds turn the sunbeam on and off during the day? The variable rays spotlighting interior surfaces is an esthetic experience to many people. Can we put a numerical value on an esthetic experience?

Fenestration — a very important word in this business of saving energy — means everything, from the design of a specific window to the relationship between all windows (voids) and walls (solids). We argue for hours about solids and voids, their exact proportions, the vistas, the good and bad effects of sun and wind. There are no pat answers, but this we do know. In our search for balance between conserving energy on one hand and protecting human values on the other:

Fenestration design requires great judgment.

Study this case, a science building in Colorado. Note the variety of windows. Consider the logic of solids and voids. We put glass where glass is needed. Where it isn't, we put walls. See Photo A: The wing on the right, a student lounge, has a magnificent view of the Rocky Mountains. So we used lots of glass. We think now we used too much. Nevertheless, if energy is precious, so is a rare view. There must be a balance. In the laboratory wing, Photo B, we used glass sparingly. It makes sense.

who can measure the value of a view of Pikes Peak?

Refer to Photo C. Function affects form. A lounge wing looks like what it is. So does a lab. In Photo D you see a profuse use of glass. Rightly so. It's a botanical greenhouse. Photo E, the west side of the laboratory, has minimum glass, but note that we set the glass deep for sun control.

The logic of solids and voids creates asymmetrical beauty.

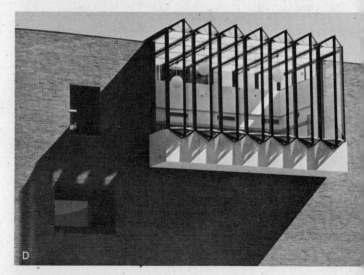

Glass is an ineffective thermal barrier. Heat flows through it with relative ease. That's why energy conscious people seem to dislike windows. Apparently they would love ice boxes, cold storage rooms and caves. But glass isn't all that bad. Double panes are pretty good to stop heat flow; certainly better than single panes but not as good as insulated walls. Reflective glass does a bang-up job of diverting the hot sun rays. Combined with double panes, reflective or mirror glass does a fair job. However, in the winter when solar radiation is needed, this solution prevents the full heating effect of the sun. Regardless whether glass is effective or ineffective as a thermal barrier, it must be used in buildings occupied by people. The trick is to use it where it will do the most good.

Glass helps to create the warm, friendly atmosphere that leads to the architectural experience.

Glass helps to humanize mere buildings — raising them to a higher plateau where human values exist. Glass provides view by bringing inside beautiful outside things. It eliminates the depressed feeling of confinement. Prisoners used to be punished by confinement in windowless space. That should tell us something. Glass is controversial, but it might well be the saving grace of human existence. We decided long before the energy crisis that it's much better to be a little cold than to have no view of snow on the ground. That it's much better to be a little warm than not to be able to see the beautiful summer green of trees and shrubs. We like natural light, the way it changes every hour. We like to work and live in spaces which are adequately lighted by the sky. We don't like the monotony of electric lighting. We like to have openings in walls to be cooled by the breeze on hot humid days. We like nature. We like to bring it into our buildings.

Glass helps to give us buildings which fulfill certain basic human needs — to see the sky, to hear a bird, to feel the breeze, to smell the flowers, to see the hills, or to look down from a high rise on an exciting urban scene. In responding to the energy shortage, which will be with us for a long time, architects, engineers, planners and their clients must remember that

buildings are for people.

Buildings are for people to play in, to rest in, to work in, to pray in, to learn in. A building must help people. It has a prime task. If that task is not done well all the insulation in the world won't help.

We can't establish a numerical value of amenities gained by looking from an inside space to an inspiring view. But the value is real. To see trees, sky, and water is fulfilling basic human needs. Man did live in caves. But he got out of them— and for good reasons. A windowless building is just a cave above the ground.

Don't send us back to the caves

An outside view creates an inside atmosphere which enriches lives. There is no doubt from the CRS experience of designing and evaluating hundreds of buildings that people respond to form and space, one way or another. We've found that the ability to look out of an enclosed space to an interesting, beautiful view affects behavior patterns—by inspiring people to do better.

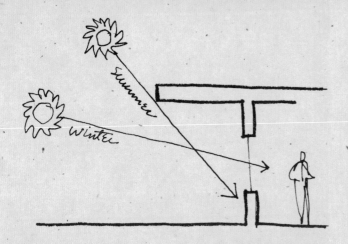

Summer sun is high; winter sun low. This allows shading devices to selectively admit the warming sun rays during the coldest months and to exclude the direct rays at the time of year when the additional heat is unwanted. The sun's path is precise and predictable. The designer uses this as an opportunity to control the sun's effect on his building. The most effective way to reduce unwanted solar transmission is to use external shading like trees, fins, overhangs or awnings, which stop solar transmission, leaving the glass in shade. Solar radiation is also transmitted by reflection from surfaces such as white building materials, glassy water and sand.

Internal devices like blinds, drapery and shades help reduce solar transmission through glass, but are less effective than external shading. Under the best conditions, internal devices can only reduce transmission by 65 percent. When direct sunlight falls on ¼" plate glass, as much as 80 percent of the sun's energy will be transmitted into the space. At night, the problem is reversed, and the drapery keeps the heat from escaping to the atmosphere while the overhang becomes ineffective. Again,

there is no single solution to use or stop solar radiation.

Each case must be handled as a specific application of sun control.

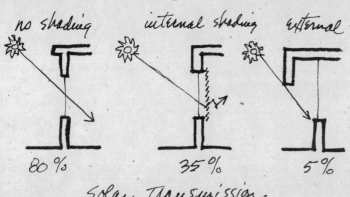

no shading   internal shading   external

80%   35%   5%

Solar Transmission

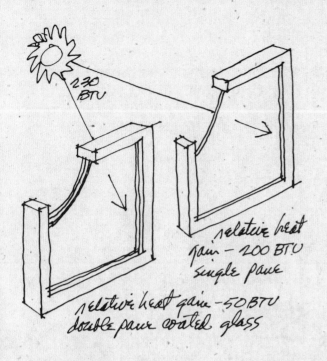

230 BTU

relative heat gain - 200 BTU single pane

relative heat gain - 50 BTU double pane coated glass

75%

25%

aluminum frame 4250 BTU heat loss per day

87%

13%

wooden frame 1450 BTU heat loss per day

Glass is great for view. Does a beautiful job of stopping the wind. Permits wanted winter solar radiation, but is a poor thermal barrier. The use of double panes and reflective surfaces, however, help to alleviate this major weakness. Compared to ¼" plate glass, double pane glass can reduce solar transmission by 10 to 15 percent in the summer, and it is twice as resistant to conductance both in the winter and summer. Double pane glass with reflective or absorptive coated surfaces can compare even more favorably, reducing transmission as much as 75 percent.

¼" plate glass allows 80 percent of the solar energy to penetrate,

about ten times the transmission of a wall, and it conducts heat from the interior to the exterior five to ten times faster than a well-insulated wall.

According to the National Bureau of Standards, 25 percent of the heat lost through an aluminum window is lost through the frame. A wood assembly loses only 13 percent through its frame. A 10 square foot aluminum window facing south will lose 4250 BTU/day in winter and will have more heat gain in summer than wood. One of several ways to solve the problem is to use an assembly with a thermal break of a material like rubber or plastic which conducts inefficiently.

The "greenhouse effect" of glass and some transparent plastics occurs because glass is transparent to certain wavelengths of light and completely opaque to radiation of long wavelengths. Radiation from the sun is admitted, absorbed by the interior surfaces, and given off as heat, which is longer wavelength radiation. Glass doesn't allow long wave radiation to escape, so the interior temperature goes higher than it would with an open window.

Controlling the sun — keeping it on the glass in winter, off in summer — is no great problem. But now that buildings must be designed to use energy more efficiently we must be more careful than ever how we locate and size windows.

Use glass to take advantage of the sun.

There are many ways to do this. Here are a few.

All-glass buildings should be rare. So should window-less buildings. But the glass wall and the solid wall can be useful and beautiful if there is logic relating to visual needs. Solid walls portray great strength, screen bad views, afford privacy, protect from sun radiation, stop heat transfer. And what better sun control for west exposures? But most important—solid wall construction gives the feeling of permanence which is so important to all of us. Beauty relates to logic.

There is beauty in blank walls

related to the intellectual idea that a wall serves a specific function. The street side of this house has no glass except the greenhouse "hat" that covers the inner court adjacent to the heated entry. The other side—the south, private side—has considerable glass for view and winter sun. Generous overhangs keep the sun off the glass in the summer. The blank walls on the north afford privacy and protection from the cold winds. Such an arrangement gives designers the opportunity to cram the wall with as much insulation as the balance of economy/energy will permit.

The photo across the page of an Alabama school is further evidence that blank walls in architectural compositions can be beautifully dramatic.

What you see here are sketches of a "solar house" which could also be a church, a clinic, an office, or anything else. It's adapted from the Trombe/Michel solar wall idea developed in France in 1956. They tell us it works. We're anxious to build one. The principle is so simple:

As the greenhouse traps sun, so do these vertical south-facing walls collect solar energy.

The sun penetrates two sheets of glass; hits and heats the black concrete wall. This wall has a high thermal capacity to store heat and provide warmth at night. There is a natural thermocirculation of air as seen in the cross sections of summer and winter operation. Also note the sliding door garage shown on the plan at right which houses moveable insulated doors that cover the "greenhouse" walls to retain the heat at night or block the summer sun at times when thermocirculation proves ineffective. If the exterior doors are pulled over the glass at night, they block the out flow of heat. Insulating drapes can be pulled over the inside wall to encourage the flow of heat into the external walls. This is a primitive type of solar house requiring considerable manual or mechanical control; nevertheless, it does have great potential in low cost facilities as a supplement to the common heating systems.

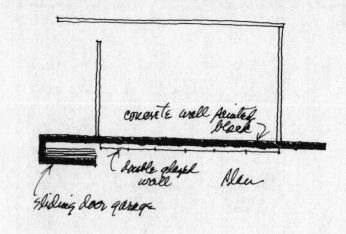

concrete wall painted black

double glazed wall   Plan

sliding door garage

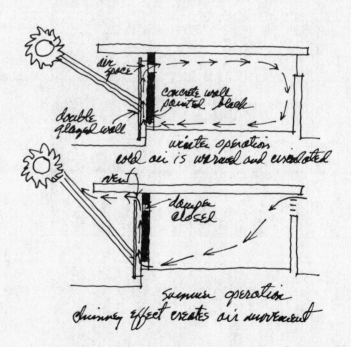

air space

concrete wall painted black

double glazed wall

winter operation
cold air is warmed and circulated

vent

damper closed

summer operation
chimney effect creates air movement

Most people think that a window lets in light, lets in air, and affords view. We have found that the common windows which do this are rarely satisfactory — that it's better to separate these three functions. In other words, a window that has one function is not compromised by the other two. For example, Photo A is of a large plastic bubble, in essence a round, horizontal window, which admits a lot of light to the lounge below. Photo B shows windows that admit air. Note that they are located at floor level so the interior air flow will be in the living zone near the floor. Photo C is a view window, used from a sitting position.

Each window has its purpose.

In the large photograph you can see a number of different kinds of windows with different functions. The protruding window that looks like the lens of a camera is strictly for view and aimed at a particular vista. The deeply inset window below it and slightly to the left has a similar function but different design and directional view. Behind these view windows are student/faculty lounges. The little windows grouped as a pair serve two faculty offices. The large vertical window serves to light the lobbies at each floor for the elevator and stairs, and provides an exterior scale by serving as an indicator of the various floors.

It cannot be overemphasized that a window is an energy control. Depending upon its design, the window controls free light energy, free wind energy, and in one sense it controls the atmosphere of interior space.

Take the windows off the outside wall and put them on the inside.

It's not a bad idea. And we've done it many times, including these projects in Illinois, Minnesota and Texas. If the use of outside glass must be kept to a minimum then inside windows like these can provide much-needed vistas. Saves energy, too.

It is becoming an established fact that

open plans consume less energy

than the conventional eggcrate partitioned layout. When the CRS team helped to bust the classroom box years ago by eliminating partitions to respond to team teaching, we told our clients that the open plan was the most efficient way to achieve cross ventilation and natural lighting. We know now that through engineering analysis and tests this also holds true for heating systems, air conditioning systems and electric lighting systems. The more open the better. These photographs are examples of the open plan concept.

If large spaces like these were subdivided box-like into many small spaces, more energy would be required. It's easy to see why: Partitions block off both light distribution and air flow. The eggcrate arrangement uses more energy and the first cost is higher since mechanical and electrical equipment must be larger. The open plan for office buildings and schools comes close to what we're looking for: a Cadillac with a Volkswagen engine.

If you want to save energy,
bury part of the building.

Earth is a good insulator. We first put this principle into practice over twenty years ago designing spaces such as auditoriums, dining rooms and gymnasiums requiring high ceilings which would disrupt the simple, economic roof lines. We told our clients, "Let's use a bulldozer and dig down to get the extra ceiling heights. We can cut construction cost and save fuel over the years."

More recently we have used earth berms to cut heat loss through walls, as the photos show. We have put many spaces underground that required no daylight or view. The performing arts halls in Houston and Akron, for example, have their rehearsal and dressing rooms underground. In both of these great halls the users' offices are partly buried. We like the idea of basement spaces with light wells and view courts to humanize them.

Thermal comfort for people varies 10 to 15 degrees, but designers can assume certain parameters. Warm and cold sensations depend upon four interrelated factors: air temperature, humidity, air movement and radiation. The American Society of Heating Refrigeration and Air Conditioning Engineers identifies a range of temperature and humidity that 80 percent of us will find comfortable. Design for the high side of comfort in summer, and low side in winter saves energy. According to the National Bureau of Standards, on a humid summer day with 50 percent relative humidity outdoors, 30 percent more cooling energy is required to maintain 50 than 60 percent indoor relative humidity. On a typical dry winter day of 10 degrees outdoors, twice as much heating energy is required to maintain 40 than 20 percent relative humidity. For further savings, the NBS recommends wearing warmer clothing in winter and lighter clothing in summer, extending the temperature range lower and higher to 68 degrees and 80 degrees. Considerable energy can be saved if we:

Design on the edge of comfort.

In the Washington, D. C. area with an average outside winter temperature of 40 degrees, each degree the thermostat is reduced saves 3 percent. A 6 degree reduction yields 18 percent in savings. In a climate with an outside average temperature of 20 degrees, as in Minnesota, there is a 2 percent savings per degree of reduction. The shaded portion of the chart indicates temperature and humidity parameters considered comfortable by ASHRAE. The dotted portion indicates extension of that range to include clothing changes. In the top photo at right, the students are dressed for warm weather comfort, while the bottom picture shows children at play in winter, dressed for cooler temperatures.

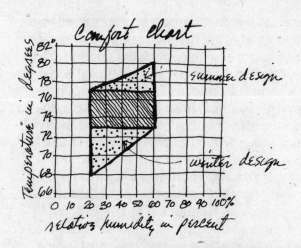

There are several mechanical systems available. They include: electric resistance heating, gas or oil fired heating, electic centrifugal cooling, absorption cooling, heat pumps, and "total energy systems". Each system has advantages. The "total energy system" is an engine driven generator on the site creating electricity and recovering engine waste heat to provide steam used in cooling and other processes. It has a thermal efficiency of 60 to 70 percent. Power from a utility company for electric heat is about 32 percent thermally efficient. Heat pump systems provide both heating and cooling. The one we used in a New Mexico school consumes one third to one fourth the energy required by electrical resistance heaters. The junior college power plant in the photo is a combination of gas fired heating and electric centrifugal cooling. Each building has different heating and cooling requirements. We must:

Select the right system for each application.

Other features allow further energy savings. Heat from lighting fixtures in some buildings is half of the cooling load. There are methods of recovering that heat for terminal reheat systems, space heating or heat storage. We built a building which takes return air out through the light troffer, carrying heat away from the space. Some heat exchange systems let us extract heat from exhaust air to warm incoming fresh air with 60 percent efficiency. Since trash has one fourth the heating value of coal, Nashville generates power from solid waste. Houston buries 30,000 tons of garbage a week, a fuel potential equal to one third of Houston's electrical demand. Heat storage systems store heat during non-peak hours to be released at peak demand times, allowing smaller, more economical plants. NBS says heat

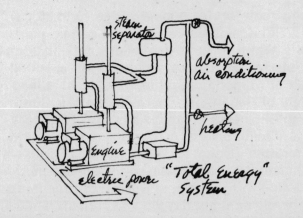

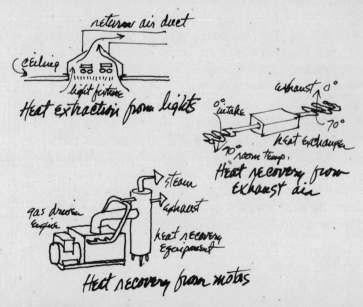

storage can cut peak loads in half, reducing energy consumption 6 percent. Body heat from people is a real factor in determining the heating/cooling load.

Waste heat can be recovered from many things—even from people.

Energy efficient systems are examples of equipment choices which help us reduce consumption. Reducing loads on the equipment also saves energy. We can reduce air changes. With proper filtering, recirculated air requires less intake air to be heated or cooled. Low velocity systems consume less energy. Where codes allow, we can cut back from 10 to 20 cubic feet/minute to 4 or 5 cubic feet/minute of forced ventilation. A well insulated building can use 55 percent less heating and cooling energy than an uninsulated building. The NBS indicates that in a well insulated structure, 36 percent of the heating and cooling is to offset infiltration. Choose the system, and design to maximize its efficiency.

Don't get caught as we did, in the awkward period of transition when our clients wanted natural ventilation that could be converted to air conditioning. It won't work.

There must be a commitment to one system—mechanical or natural ventilation.

Mechanical systems don't want a lot of holes in the envelope. Natural ventilation requires many openings to let the breeze in and out. Choose an efficient mechanical system with back-up natural ventilation, or a carefully designed natural ventilation system with mechanical back-up. Recognize that in either case, the secondary system cannot be completely efficient.

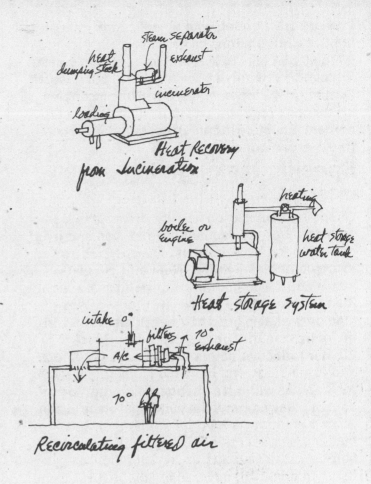

Heat Recovery from Incineration

Heat Storage System

Recirculating filtered air

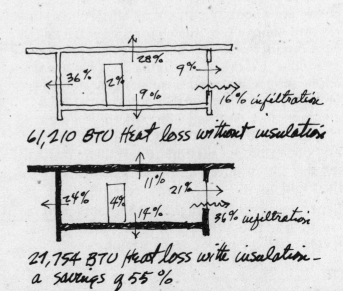

61,210 BTU Heat loss without insulation

21,754 BTU Heat loss with insulation — a savings of 55%

Low general lighting with specific high intensity light at work stations reduces electric demand 20 to 50 percent. To light an area uniformly at 70 footcandles requires 6 watts/ sq. ft., but general lighting of 40 footcandles with 70 footcandles on the task requires only 3 watts/ sq. ft., a 50 percent reduction in energy consumption. Therefore, we can conclude:

Specific task lighting saves energy.

Choosing illumination levels is important. Using 50 instead of 150 footcandles reduces energy consumption by 90 percent. The photo shows an example of task lighting. Note that circulation space and the conference room require less light than the area where people are drafting. We provide only what is needed for each task. The variety enhances the architectural experience. Lighter reflective colors on walls, ceiling, floor and furnishings can increase illumination by 30 footcandles without a change in lighting. 30 percent of some commercial buildings' electric consumption is for parking lot lighting, exterior building and security flood lights. Reduction in lighting reduces loads on air conditioning systems. In some commercial buildings, heat from lights is one half the cooling load. Incandescent lamps are about 30 percent as efficient as fluorescent lamps. The chart shows approximate light output in lumens per watt of several types of lighting. Color and size limitations mean each application must be considered separately. High voltage distribution carries more power on a single circuit. Fixtures with better diffusers or lenses contribute to efficiency by reducing glare and giving proper distribution. Multiple switching permits turning off unused portions of the building.

Separately switched night lighting sufficient for cleaning and security at 5 to 10 percent of normal levels is an off-peak energy savings.

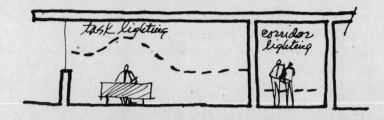

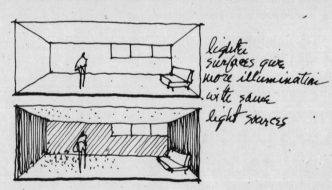

lighter surfaces give more illumination with same light sources

Light sources	Lumens/watt
incandescent bulbs	75
quartz lamps	20
mercury vapor	35
fluorescent tubes	65
metal halide	80
high pressure sodium	100

The energy crisis has caused a renewed interest in natural light. We know very little, however, about how building forms respond to daylight. What does an overhang do to light distribution? Skylights? Ground reflection? Study these little sketches and you can see:

How natural light responds to form.

Look at Sketch A. The space is unilaterally lighted — a window on one side only. Note the light near the window. Not much near the opposite wall. Now go to Sketch B. An overhang has been added. Also a skylight near the solid wall. Note the light curve. Although light intensity is lowered somewhat near the window, the distribution is straightened out and considerably better. And now to Sketch C: By increasing the ground reflection, light bounces to the ceiling and raises the illumination near the overhang. In Sketch D the skylight is eliminated and a second window and overhang are added, providing an excellent bilaterally lighted space — nearly a straight line distribution curve. The overhangs are sun controls which keep hot summer suns away from glass. They also help to provide a better quality of lighting, free from direct sun and sky glare.

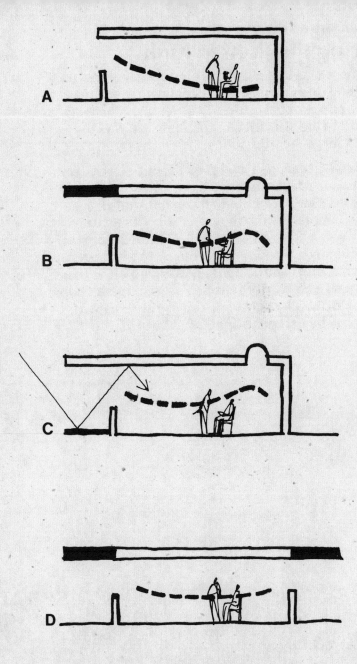

If you are able to use natural light,
bring the light in high.

A mere two-foot slit at the connection of wall and ceiling does a great job of lighting the spaces. See photo of the house. The clerestory arrangement in the student lounge photo is a way to light large, interior spaces.

The CRS team has designed spaces so you can't tell where daylight stops and electric lighting begins. See the photo of the school hallway, as an example. During the day, the lights are rarely turned on. In another school, the classrooms are lighted by a plenum which mixes and integrates natural and electric lighting, directed through an eggcrate ceiling (required to prevent glare and provide quality lighting). You can save a lot of energy by using the light from the sky.

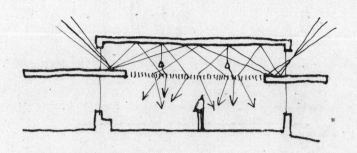

Cross ventilation was a common phrase a decade ago. Air conditioning just about erased it from our vocabulary. Why use the wind to cool when we had abundant cheap fuel? But now the wind is very popular. Certainly natural ventilation doesn't do as good a cooling job as air conditioning. But it uses no energy. In the 50's we learned a lot about:

How the wind behaves within a space.

We need now to review what we learned. How to conserve fuel. How to supplement air conditioning with natural ventilation. These sketches will give you a rough idea how air flow from the wind is affected by building form. What you see in Sketch A is a bilaterally vented envelope. The pattern of the air flow is upward, caused by the ground effect and the solid walls. That's a good way to take the heat off the ceiling, but air flows over people's heads. So it has minimum cooling effect. In Sketch B an overhang has been added which forces the air down and around people. Now refer to Sketch C. If the overhang is moved to the window head, the air will flow upward again. This kind of wind behavior surprises most people. It's nearly impossible to predetermine the exact pattern, mathematically. We use empirical judgment. Sometimes we use models. By relocating the window on the leeward wall, shown in Sketch D, the air still flows upward over the heads of people and down the wall. It would seem that the air would flow directly from one window to another, which isn't necessarily so. A window is like a nozzle that controls direction of the air. The size of the opening controls the velocity.

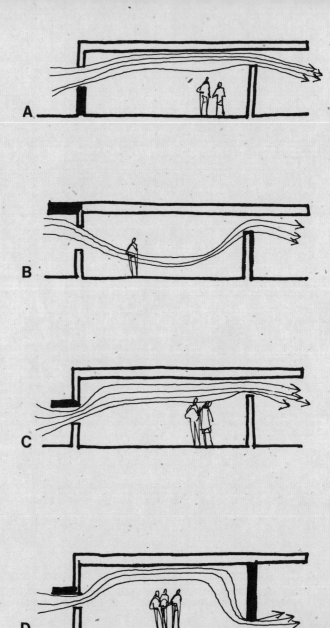

50

Evaporative coolers are often used to maintain a cool, dust-free atmosphere in hot, arid regions. The basic evaporative cooler unit—a poor man's air conditioner—is a container of absorbent wood excelsior which is kept moist. A fan draws outside air through the excelsior where dust is filtered out and the temperature is lowered. See sketch. The cool air forces the hot air out of the window vents. Although the temperature is not reduced greatly, the moisture in the air provides a sensation of coolness.

Before air conditioning, evaporative coolers were very popular.

We may see more of them in the future because they use very little energy.

This is a little school in Laredo, Texas, on the Mexican border. Natural ventilation is not appropriate there because the summer winds are too hot. Air conditioning is preferred over evaporative coolers, of course, but cooling with moisture and filtering out the dust is better than nothing at all.

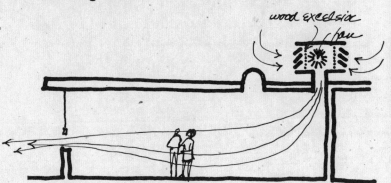

there is nothing quite like a porch

When the wind is bad, it's bad. When it's good it's good. It can be quite good at times in the summer. That's why someone way back there invented the porch. That's why the old possum run or dog trot houses in the south and southwest still provide comfort. On a recent trip to the warm region of Russia, we saw some dog trot houses with a breezeway that funnels and accelerates the wind. It is still a good idea. No air conditioning system has yet been able to duplicate the effect of a fresh breeze.

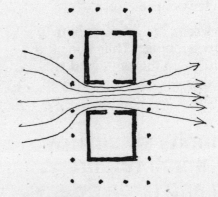

Here's how the wind flows over and through a building. When it blows against a building (A), it creates a high pressure area. As it blows over and around the building there is created on the leeward side a low pressure (B) area often referred to as a wind shadow. If openings were made in both the windward and leeward walls, it would have a push-pull effect, forcing the air into the building from one side and sucking it out from the other (C). Air, of course, flows from high pressure to low pressure areas. This is great when you want the cool breeze. But in the cold weather, when you don't want the wind to blow on you, it can be quite comfortable even outdoors sitting in a sunny wind shadow. Nature knew what it was doing. In most regions the wind direction is reversed from summer to winter — permitting the sun to shine in the wind shadows. That's why courts are feasible year round.

Most people have the wrong idea about where to locate and size window openings. They think the large openings should be on the windward side to scoop the air in. Quite wrong. That is if you want substantial airflow. It will just dam up on the inside.

Maximum velocity of airflow occurs when small openings are windward and large openings are leeward.

With this arrangement the airflow will have a greater velocity than the wind itself.

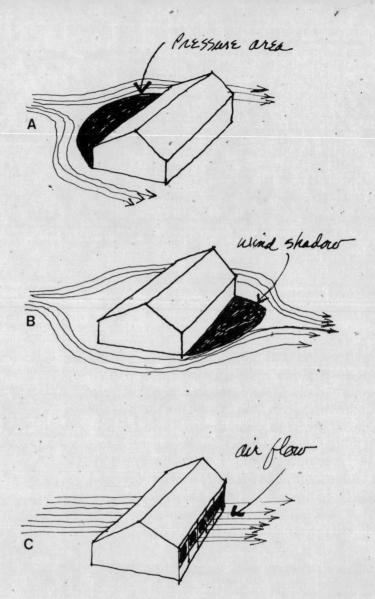

The Gulf Coast region is particularly adaptable to natural ventilation. During the hot months there is generally a breeze. When this breeze blows around the body on hot humid days, there is a sensation of coolness. This little school is unique in that by the use of pressure walls the back-to-back classroom will have adequate air flow.

Pressure walls create high and low pressure areas.

Since air flows from high pressure to low pressure, we create our own micro climate, our own inside wind.

The pressure walls, as indicated in the plan diagram, divert and force the air to flow into and through the leeward classrooms. There is an esthetic quality about these freestanding walls that is reminiscent of Mies van der Rohe's Barcelona Pavilion. Natural ventilation gives logic to form.

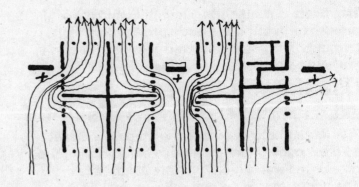

Wind helps. Wind hurts. On hot, humid days, air movement around the body provides comfort. On cold, windy days, the wind goes right through you. So what we want to do is:

Use the wind when it's needed. Get out of it when it's not.

The large photo is a school on the Gulf Coast where a cooling breeze always blows during the nine or ten warm months. Note the double roof. The upper roof is an umbrella, protecting the buildings and children from rain and hot sun. The breeze flowing between the two roofs removes hot air. The hot sun rarely reaches the walls and never reaches the second roof. Louvered windows near the floor line provide cross ventilation. Classrooms are daylighted. We used the free energy from both the sky and the wind.

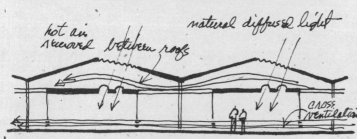

The lower picture is another school with a unique natural ventilation system for back-to-back classrooms. The windward rooms are raised to allow air to flow underneath to the classrooms on the leeward side. The upper set of louvered air inlets serves the front row of classrooms, and the lower set serves the leeward rooms. We goofed a bit by providing cross

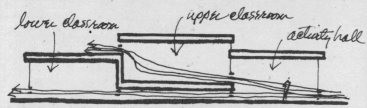

ventilation in an area where the winds are too hot most of the time. Evaporative cooling might have been better.

Ventilation is affected by plant materials. Air crossing hard reflective or absorptive surfaces like parking lots and sidewalks is warmed, but air passing through trees and plants will be cooled. The winter wind can be blocked by plant material, especially evergreens and plants with heavy foliage. CRS often designs planting with deciduous trees on the south which cool the air in summer and drop their leaves to let in precious sunlight in winter. We use thicker evergreen types on northern exposures to break the cold wind.

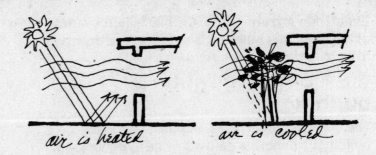

air is heated

air is cooled

Different climates require different designs.

The school children in the photo are comfortable on a relatively cold day, sitting in the sun protected by a free-standing wind break. In hot dry climates, it is best to keep the wind out of the inside spaces. Moisture is needed for a cooling sensation. But in warm humid situations, the air movement provided by ventilation makes us feel cool. In cold weather, winds are unwanted. Buildings do well to turn their backs to the wind in northern areas. Energy is saved by respecting the climate.

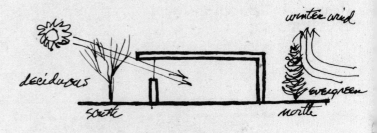

deciduous

south

winter wind

evergreen

north

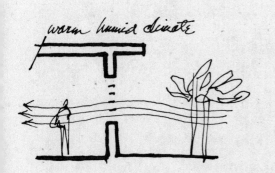

warm humid climate

hot dry climate

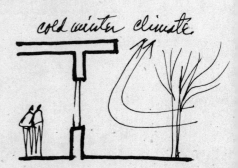

cold winter climate

Located in Arizona where the sun is fierce much of the time, this building is wrapped in a desert robe to resist the heat. Actually,

it's a building within a building.

The outside "robe" covering the inner steel building is concrete painted white to deflect the sun's rays. There is space between the two which is ventilated by the wind.

This Pennsylvania building saves energy through a plan arrangment which we call

thermal buffer zone.

The zone is a peripheral corridor occupying over 20 percent of the total floor area and separating the interior seated-activity space from the outside walls. This works on the notion that people tolerate lower and higher temperatures when moving.

Consider summer cooling. Assume that outside temperature is 95 degrees and that 76 degree temperature is desired in the interior activity space. Moving people could easily tolerate 81 degrees because they create their own breeze and don't stay in the corridor very long. So the cooling system only needs to drop the temperature to 81 degrees instead of all the way down to 76. This might even be accomplished by natural ventilation. Windows are controls, just like switches and thermostats.

Now let's consider winter heating. If the thermal buffer zone corridor were oriented for sun penetration creating a greenhouse effect, resulting heat could serve the interior activity space. The peripheral corridor also stops infiltration into the interior spaces—and saves energy. Assume that the outside temperature is zero and 68 degrees is needed in the seated activity space. Users could tolerate 63 degrees in the corridor. By closing windows, using the sun and small amounts of energy, this can be accomplished. Then the heating system needn't work as hard to heat the seated activity space.

The thermal zone recognizes that certain tasks require less or more heating than other tasks.

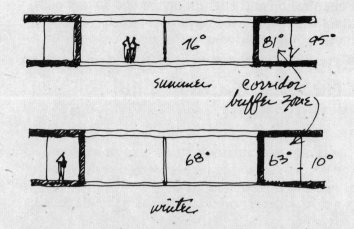

Fenestration and orientation are two salient considerations for saving energy. In this case, a bank/office in Galveston, Texas:

Energy was saved by proper orientation and logical fenestration.

There are no windows on the west and east. Glass on the south exposure is protected from the hot sun during the summer by deeply inset windows. We reduced the solar heat load by 20 percent when we oriented the main facade to the south instead of the west. We reduced by 25 percent the first cost of the heating/air conditioning system when we decided not to build a typical glass office tower. And we reduced by almost 50 percent the amount of fuel used each year.

In the case of our own office building in Houston where we have continuous glass around the entire perimeter so that our people can fully appreciate the magnificent views, we saved 25 percent of the cooling load by using large overhangs 20 feet on the west and east, and 10

feet on the south. We don't know how much these overhangs cut down the wind loads in the winter, but we do know that the surrounding trees have a very significant effect on saving energy. Another interesting aspect of this project is the cooling effect of our cars parked on the roof above. They make excellent umbrellas, providing shade for the building.

The main question concerning proper orientation and the design of fenestration is simply this: What do we do with the hole in the box? Whatever we do is a trade-off. But that's design. Call it total balance, or the beautiful compromise. But in the process of designing windows in terms of type, function, exposure, location, size, we seek the balance between optimum energy use and fulfillment of human needs.

Sun control on east and west elevations can be achieved, but with difficulty. This college building (right) shows an effective way.

The windows are arranged in a sawtooth, oblique fashion providing north exposure for each window.

Note that each of the three floors has different plans, each relating to specific functional requirements. The sketch is of the second floor. These planar forms are beautiful and energy saving.

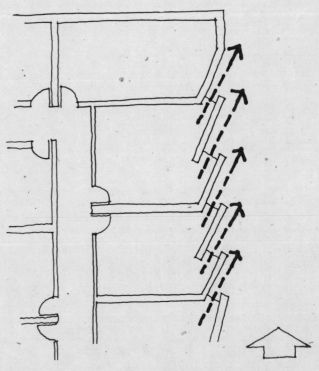

The hotel shown on the left has used a sawtooth design to focus on a fine downtown view while protecting against the severe western sun.

Energy saving exterior devices can keep the sun from entering a building through glass during the hot months, but permit it to penetrate during the cold months. The common overhang works exceedingly well on south exposures, but is not very effective in keeping the sun off west and east exposures. Vertical baffles are better. The ideal arrangement for southwest and southeast exposures seems to be a combination of the two — an eggcrate arrangement. The photo on the left shows one of the many adaptations of the eggcrate-type sun control. The photo on the right might be classified as a pure form of the overhang.

CITY HALL ANNEX

This college in Southern California is a good example of the step-back method used to control the sun. The upper floors serve as overhangs to shade the lower floors. The soffit must be well insulated to insure against heat transfer.

This college in Illinois is fortunate. It owns its own water and trees. Buildings respond with glass walls for the students and faculty to enjoy the magnificent views. However, these views are toward the south. So there is a problem of the sun overheating the buildings during the hot months. This is solved by the use of a combination of overhangs and baffles. Keeping the summer sun off the glass reduces the cooling load. During the winter months, sun on glass is desirable for thermal comfort.

We are very excited about the future. Just as system building, construction systems, fast track, and construction management gave impetus to the CRS team, so has "design for energy" brought new thoughts and a fresh approach to solving problems. Like the evolution which occurred in CRS of a new esthetic reflecting building systems, so we feel there will be a similar evolution in the search for new forms to reflect the new ethic of energy conservation. We are particularly excited about the fact that

new energy sources will bring new forms.

Housing, schools, hospitals, and other building types will begin to take on different silhouettes. The great designers will be inspired by the engineering honesty of the solar collectors and will find ways to express them as elements that help cause the architectural experience to happen. These new forms will be appreciated for their beauty as well as for their economic use of energy. The National Bureau of Standards estimates that a 40 by 14 foot solar collector panel combined with a 150,000 BTU heat storage water tank can save 40 percent of an average residence's heating energy in the Washington, D.C. area.

There are still problems with the "solar house". One of these pertains to the hardware. It will pay for itself in the long run, but this may take ten years. And, the hardware is hard to get. The solar house will catch on when manufacturers can profit by producing the hardware, and when architects and engineers can go to Sweet's Catalog to find it.

The design profession will meet the challenge of the energy crisis. And we will produce better, more meaningful and more appreciated buildings.

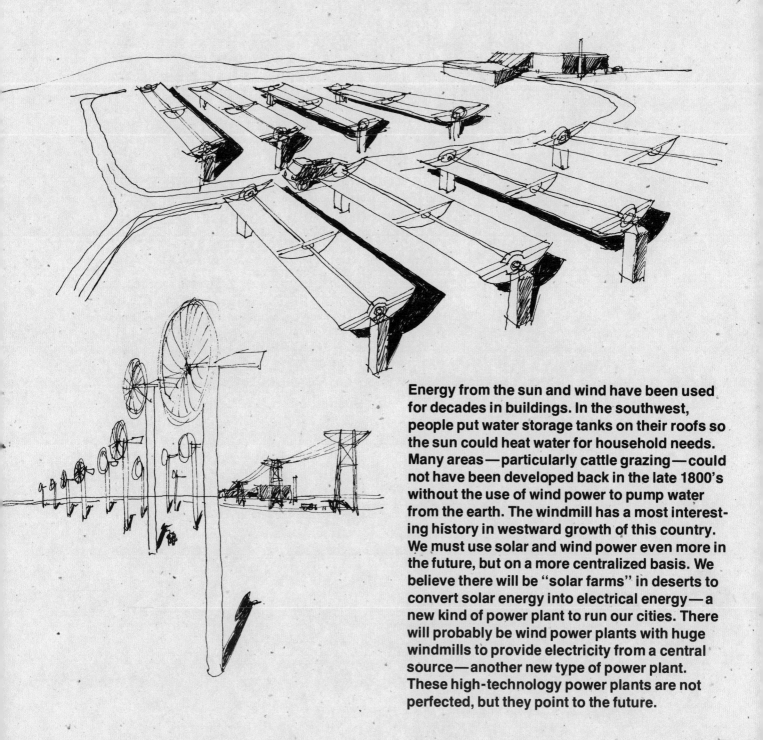

Energy from the sun and wind have been used for decades in buildings. In the southwest, people put water storage tanks on their roofs so the sun could heat water for household needs. Many areas—particularly cattle grazing—could not have been developed back in the late 1800's without the use of wind power to pump water from the earth. The windmill has a most interesting history in westward growth of this country. We must use solar and wind power even more in the future, but on a more centralized basis. We believe there will be "solar farms" in deserts to convert solar energy into electrical energy—a new kind of power plant to run our cities. There will probably be wind power plants with huge windmills to provide electricity from a central source—another new type of power plant. These high-technology power plants are not perfected, but they point to the future.

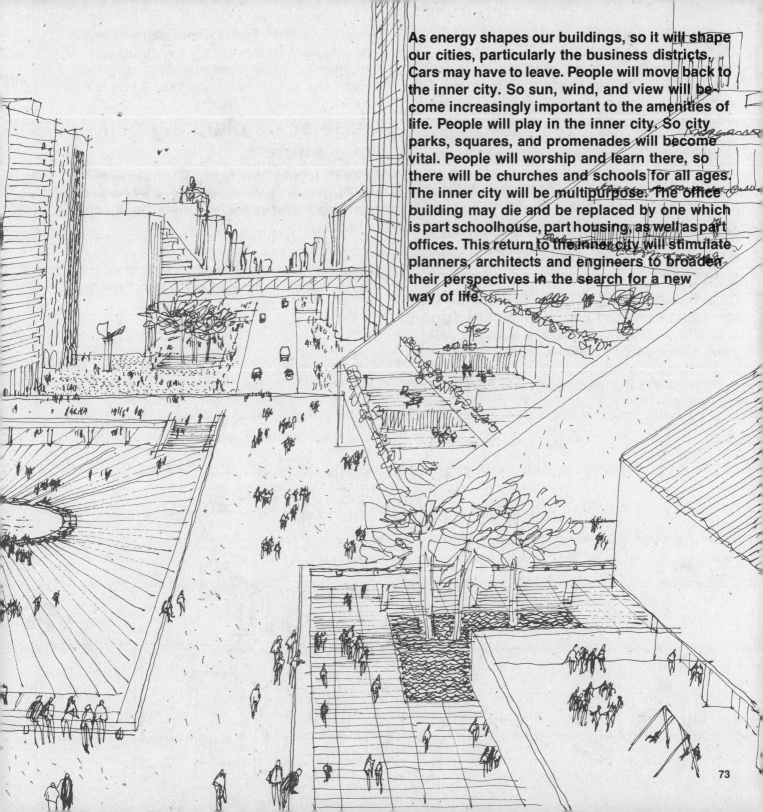

As energy shapes our buildings, so it will shape our cities, particularly the business districts. Cars may have to leave. People will move back to the inner city. So sun, wind, and view will become increasingly important to the amenities of life. People will play in the inner city. So city parks, squares, and promenades will become vital. People will worship and learn there, so there will be churches and schools for all ages. The inner city will be multipurpose. The office building may die and be replaced by one which is part schoolhouse, part housing, as well as part offices. This return to the inner city will stimulate planners, architects and engineers to broaden their perspectives in the search for a new way of life.

73

New Franconia is a proposed new town for 35,000 people on a 1,850 acre site in Fairfax County, Virginia. In many ways, New Franconia anticipated the energy crisis. The town was designed around high density residential nodes separated by green belts. Each of the nodes is tied to a people-moving system. This system will be tied to the Washington Metro when it is completed. Consequently all of the town centers and the city of Washington are convenient without the use of an automobile.

All schools will have direct access to the mobility system.

Other transportation will not be needed. This will eliminate busing and free students from rigid school bus schedules, allowing them to participate in after-school activities, special programs and resources available at other schools in the system, and to use community and District of Columbia facilities.

Obviously a town that is integrated and organized around a contemporary transportation system saves great quantities of money and energy. But even more important, it would provide a better way of living.

Large scale planning can save energy.

Large residential areas, multipurpose complexes, resorts, and particularly new towns, offer great opportunities for new methods of conservation.

Spaces which serve many people, such as the college campus shown at right and many urban spaces, consume smaller amounts of energy.

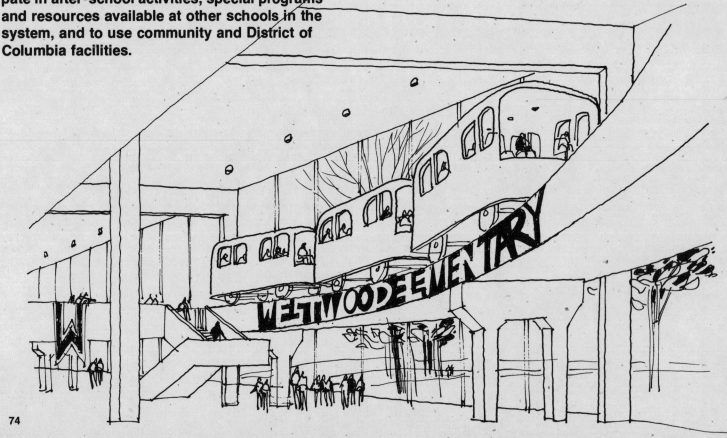

Urban interior spaces, like giant hotel lobbies, shopping malls, underground pedestrian walks and overstreet bridges, museums and halls for the performing arts, are efficient.

The amount of energy used per person decreases.

The great halls present interesting problems in the conservation of energy. Answers lie in the programming of such halls. Should the building be designed for the year's peak crowd, or for average attendance? If it's designed for three thousand and the average attendance is one thousand, there is much energy wasted. Great judgment must be exerted during the programming stage to determine the optimum size. Innovations are needed to provide flexibility in mechanical and electrical systems which can adapt the facility to the size of the audience and avoid wasting energy.

Consider energy use in outside urban spaces like pedestrian streets, plazas, promenades, garden and fountain areas, outside lobbies, sidewalk cafes, and parking areas. Again, answers lie in the programming of these spaces to consider task lighting, and even task heating and task cooling.

In CRS we have a term we use quite often:

Conditioned outdoor spaces.

These are patios and courts, corridors, play sheds, and the like. The conditioning of outdoor spaces makes a lot of sense, if properly designed. They cost less and use less energy than indoor spaces. Conditioning the outdoors is a concept. Let's look at kinds of outdoor spaces. The upper left photo is a college in Illinois. What we see is a conditioned academic street. Everyone is there between classes. It's protected from the winter winds — actually a sun pocket. And no precious energy is wasted. A bargain.

The lower left photo is also a college. This is in Arizona. The main concourse is Academic Town Square where students and faculty gather. Note the protection from uncomfortable hot winds in summer and cold winds in winter. If these outside corridors were air conditioned and heated, the first cost of the building would have been increased some twenty percent and much energy would be wasted. The upper right photo is a civic center in Texas, another example of conditioned space. Its court provides a pleasant atmosphere for activities including dining, and is usable many days of the year. It is conditioned to protect its users from strong winds from the plains.

The lower right photo is of an elementary school in Alabama. In the winter it provides a sun pocket protected from the cold winds and in the summer plenty of shade for the kids. Note the accented air intake. Also the extensive use of glass on the east side with very little on the west. There is a definite relationship between inside space and conditioned outside space.

Shelters save energy.
Open shelters cost a lot less energy and money than heated space. With an umbrella-like roof to provide sun and rain protection, many activities can be conducted better outside than inside.

Courts save energy.

If people do some of their living/working
in conditioned outdoor spaces, substantial savings in energy will be possible. A successful
court saves energy and provides a more humanistic environment than a heated, completely
enclosed room. There are many unsuccessful
courts, and we have contributed our share.
Here are photos of four highly successful,
energy saving courts.

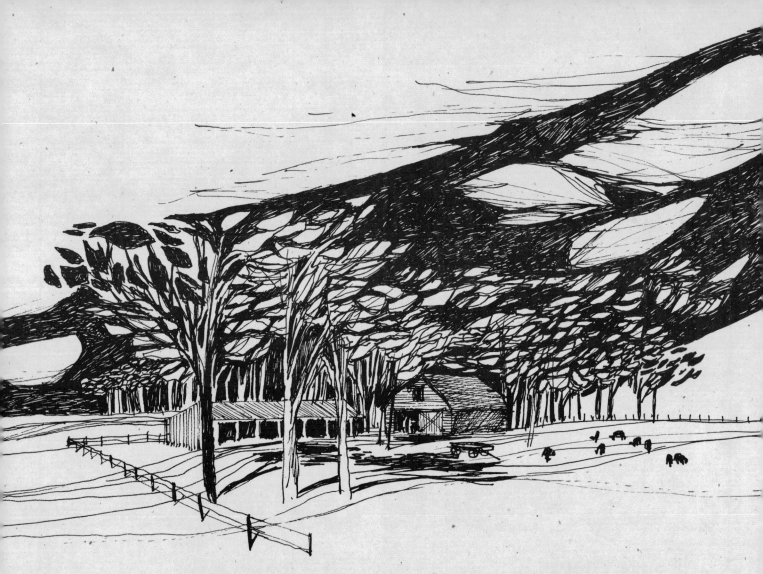

Poets praise the wind. Heating engineers hate it. It's wonderful in summer when the breeze is cooling. It seems to bite you in the winter. For sure it's something to be reckoned with. Long ago farmers who lived close to nature learned things about the wind that we should know now. They learned that the wind can jump a tree group. Farmers built their houses and animal shelters in these wind shadows. In the Franklin D. Roosevelt period, social planners took advantage of this idea and planted tree belts all over the country.

Claims were made then that when houses were placed in these wind-protected areas, as much as twenty percent of the fuel cost was saved. The farmers' cows got smart way back there, too. They turned their tails to the wind and huddled close together to form their own wind shadows. Huddling buildings together is a good idea, too. In New York State we planned an entire campus with buildings huddled together, turning tails to the wind.

We can learn a lot by studying two college buildings, somewhat similar in function. See the next two pages. One building is in Southern California (left); the other is in Massachusetts (right). Look them over very carefully. Why?

Climate shapes buildings.

The one on the left has a lot of windows, deeply inset. The other has very few. One makes use of the outdoors with outside corridors and classrooms—generically a warm weather building. The other has all heated spaces—a cold weather building.

83

We can learn how to save energy—
how best to use a bucket of oil.
We have the technology.

Can we learn to fulfill the needs of
the human being at the same time?

Credits

Associate Architects:
Donald A. Bailey and Associates
Robert O. Biering
William E. Blurock
Collins-Wagner
Dalton, Van Dijk, Johnson and Partners
Drover, Welch & Lindlan
Durrant, Deininger, Dommer, Kramer, Gordon
Fitch, Larocca, Carington, Jones
Friedman, Jobusch and Wilde
Wm. C. Haldeman
Hannon/Daniel
James M. Hartley
Koetter, Tharp & Cowell
A. A. Leyendecker
Max D. Lovett
Neuhaus & Taylor
Kenneth, Pardue, Morrison & Dean
Tom Price
Selden/Stewart
Kern Smith and Associates
Smithey & Boyd
Toughstone & Biggers
Everett Tozier

Photographers:
John Bintliff
Hedrick Blessing
Lois Bowen
Bert Brandt
James Brett
Roland Chatman
Robert Damora
Rick Gardner
Alexandre Georges
Bob Hawks
Balthazar Korab
Rush J. McCoy
McKoon Photography
Ulric Meisel
Herta Merwin
Jay Oistad
Jim Parker
Ron Partridge
Richard Payne
Ben Schnall
Dale Sedgwick
Julius Shulman
Ed Stewart
Texas Highway Department
Lawrence S. Williams
Geoff Winningham